Say it with Flowers and Plants

Ann Childs & Stanley Coleman

in association with the British Flowers and Plants Council

illustrated by Richard Fowler

AVENEL BOOKS
New York

INTRODUCTION

'If you have two pennies left in the world, spend one on a loaf of bread to keep you alive, and the other on a bunch of flowers to give you a reason for living.' Although 'pennies' are now out of date this philosophy still holds good and has induced us to compile this book.

Our aim has been to provide a quick, easy guide to buying flowers and plants, their care and using them to enhance your home. We do not pretend to be comprehensive – there are many other works that could make that claim – but we have set down the basic facts and practical hints which will enable you to prolong their life.

Flowers and plants are excellent bargains nowadays as their prices have shown relatively small increases during the last twenty-five years. If you are about to buy some, then this is the book for you and we hope that, with this simple guide, you will derive much more enjoyment from your flowers and plants.

Ann Childs and Stanley Coleman

Clearly, flowers have more than one language: there is the language with which the flowers speak to us, and the language with which we invest flowers when we use them to convey our messages.

Throughout the ages, flowers have been associated with the emotions – with sentiment, for instance, as revealed when the remains of a rose were discovered folded in an Elizabethan document, over four hundred years old.

In Victorian times, we find that flowers were endowed with many meanings; few escape mention in the little books that survive from the period. So complete are some of these that one could almost write a letter by sending a bouquet – and not always a love-letter! You could declare war with Achillea, bewail forsaken poverty with Anemones, and accuse the recipient of falsehood and crime with Tamarisk and yellow Lilies.

Needless to say, there is a brighter side to the meanings attached to flowers, many of which are just as applicable today.

The Bridal Rose   Happy love

Calceolaria   Keep this for my sake

White Chrysanthemum   Absolute truth and fidelity

Red Chrysanthemum   I love you

Daffodil   You are high in my regard

Iris   A messenger

Ivy   Faithful friendship

Fuchsia   Impeccable taste

Geranium   Friendship and comfort

Gladioli   A strong character

Daisy   Innocence of youth

Fern   Utter sincerity

Forget-me-not   Pure love

Lily of the Valley   Restored happiness

Nasturtium   Patriotic sentiment

Paeony   Shy and bashful

Snowdrop   Hopefulness

Stock   Lasting beauty

Tulip   A declaration of love

Violet   Faithful to the end

Wallflower   Fidelity

Flowers can speak for you or to you.
Enjoy them which way you will. They
are a precious part of our environment.

Special Occasions

Whatever the occasion, flowers carry a living message from giver to recipient. They respond as they are cared for, they capture attention, they are part of the household and, when they have gone, they are missed.

CHRISTMAS

A season for rejoicing – Christ's birthday. Remember the special touch that flowers can provide, at home, in a place of worship or in hospital. Chrysanthemums and Carnations are particularly lovely at this season, while spring flowers, Daffodils, Tulips, Iris and Freesias, remind us of better days ahead. Among the plants, Poinsettias, Azaleas, Cyclamen and Heathers combine colour with long-lasting qualities, and foliage plants are available in plenty for more permanent decoration.

MOTHER'S DAY

Mother's Day is celebrated at different times throughout the world. Flowers are the traditional gift for mother: spring flowers such as Daffodils, Tulips, Iris and Anemones, Freesias and Violets and Snowdrops are all very acceptable, while flowering plants such as Primulas, Calceolarias, Cinerarias and Azaleas will be equally appropriate for mothers of all ages. African Violets, too – perhaps the most appropriate plant of all.

EASTER

Spring flowers are with us in plenty at Easter, including the later varieties of Daffodils and Narcissus, mid-season Tulips and Freesias, plus the new-season's crop of Roses and Carnations. Among a wide range of plants the Hydrangeas are available. For church decoration, white Easter Lilies are the loveliest of all, complemented perhaps by white Pheasant's Eye Narcissus.

THANK YOU

So often we are on the receiving end of generosity, kindness and hospitality from those about us. To express our thanks with a gift of flowers adds grace and sincerity to our appreciation.

VALENTINE'S DAY

Be my Valentine: you cannot say this without flowers – flowers from heart to heart, a simple message that no words can supplant. Traditionally, Red Roses are *the* flowers, although red Carnations, red Chrysanthemums or any red flowers are appropriate; indeed, many other flowers may be trusted to carry your thoughts – notably Freesias, Violets or a simple posy of mixed spring flowers.

FATHER'S DAY

In many parts of the world, Father's Day is celebrated in mid-June. Father may or may not appreciate an arrangement of cut-flowers but he can be guaranteed to enjoy a gift of a plant for his office or one which can go into the garden after flowering indoors. A Hydrangea, some choice Pelargoniums or Fuchsias or some specimen Begonias could put you right with Dad for another year.

SECRETARY'S WEEK

Secretary's Week gives us an opportunity to show our appreciation for the loyalty and devotion that so many of us enjoy in our business lives. There is no easier way of saying thank you than with some suitable gift of flowers or perhaps a plant. Generally ladies prefer flowers – perhaps a choice arrangement or a bouquet that can be taken home – whilst men are more likely to enjoy a specimen foliage plant or a planted bowl.

GET WELL SOON

In no other place are flowers more appreciated than in hospital or at the side of someone who is ill. They are a comfort when conversation is impossible and their therapeutic influence is undeniable. If you make or buy a hospital arrangement, remember that it may have to go on a bedside table and should therefore not be too large. It must also have a firm base so as not to tip over easily. For the very sick, or those recovering from an operation, cool, restful colours such as pale blue or primrose are more suitable than reds and oranges. Perfumed flowers are always popular, Freesias particularly.

Weddings

No matter how far one looks back into history, no matter whose family album is opened, flowers have always been part of a wedding. In medieval times, brides wore or carried garlands of flowers. Roses or rose petals were showered upon the summer bride before confetti came into fashion. Bouquets of every style, size and fashion have their day and then return again and again.

You only need to turn the pages of any appropriate magazine published in the last hundred years to see how fashion has swung about. Today's bride is perhaps most fortunate of all. Modern florists have revived the best of the old designs and have created many new ones. The choice is enormous – not only for the bride herself but for the bridesmaids, matron of honour and the mothers, for bridegroom and best man, pages and ushers, for church, cars and reception.

Space does not allow us to show all these ideas here, but your florist can and will help you with your final choice.

CORSAGES
The mother of both bride and groom should have really special flowers that complement their outfits. It is very smart, too, to wear flowers either on your wedding hat or handbag.

BOUTONNIERES
For bridegroom, father of the bride, the best man and ushers.

LYNDA
A semi-crescent design emphasized with unusual foliage. Grey Eucalyptus Populus with five large Begonia Rex leaves underline the basic elegance of Tulips. For a lighter effect, add several trails of Stephanotis, Freesia or Hyacinth, though Roses are lovely by themselves.

CHRISTINE
A particularly graceful bouquet with movement and delicate outline. Spray Chrysanthemum is in season all the year round – hence its name, A.Y.R. Different varieties, shapes and colours come in season by season. Foliage from Scindapsus 'Marble Queen' is very effective with white, yellow and amber varieties. With pinks or dark mauve, a few leaves of Begonia Rex look magnificent.

6

JULIET

Flowers for bridesmaids should always complement their gowns so as to make a pleasing colour picture. A pomander or flower ball can be made to suit the tiniest flower girl, or it could be larger for the adult bridesmaid. Illustrated is a medium-sized design of Carnation petals trimmed with tiny rosebuds and finished with three stems of Lily-of-the-Valley.

JAYNE

A basket is light and easy to hold, looks charming and also makes a delightful table decoration for the wedding breakfast. Flowers on their natural stems are arranged in damp foam so that the design can be long-lasting. Baskets vary in size; choose one with a fairly high handle, leaving plenty of space for the flowers.

CHURCH FLOWERS

It is usually better to have a few large arrangements rather than several smaller designs. So much careful design goes into planning a wedding that the picture will not be complete without flowers in the church.

THE WEDDING CAKE

This is usually decorated with flowers that match the bridal bouquet. This lovely all-white cake is topped with a slender vase of Carole (pink) Roses and Lily-of-the-Valley. The table is decorated with narrow white satin ribbons and knots of Carole Roses joined together with Ivy foliage.

The cake top could be made on a small block of floral foam without a vase and would look just as lovely.

7

Anniversaries

Tradition describes many wedding anniversaries in terms of a present suitable for the occasion. Why no one now seems to know, but at least the list helps to solve those permanent gift problems!

1st paper	10th tin	35th coral
2nd cotton	11th steel	40th ruby
3rd leather	12th silk	45th sapphire
4th flowers	13th lace	50th gold
5th wood	14th ivory	55th emerald
6th candy	15th crystal	60th diamond
7th wool	20th china	70th platinum
8th pottery	25th silver	
9th willow	30th pearl	

No matter which anniversary you are celebrating, flowers will always grace the occasion. Here are a few ideas for the more important milestones along the path of marital bliss.

◁ Four – Flowers
Orchids, or gorgeous red roses, or a simple mixture tied with ribbon – what could be more suitable for the floral wedding anniversary!

Forty-five – Sapphire
The spray Chrysanthemums in pale amber make a striking contrast with the cocktail shaker and glasses in sapphire blue overlaid with silver; the design is highlighted with some short stems of golden Privet.

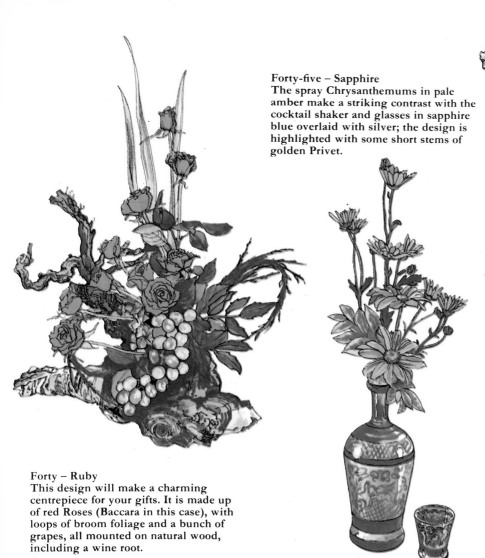

Fifty – Gold
Rather than a conventional container, use two decorative stones to display your gift, a brooch made from a gold nugget studded with sapphires. Make sure that one of the stones has a flat surface. Soak a small block of floral foam in water, and then attach it with sellotape to the flat surface. Rest the other stone neatly on top and fix the brooch to it with a small piece of plastic adhesive. Yellow Roses will highlight the presentation.

Forty – Ruby
This design will make a charming centrepiece for your gifts. It is made up of red Roses (Baccara in this case), with loops of broom foliage and a bunch of grapes, all mounted on natural wood, including a wine root.

9

Flowers of the Zodiac

AQUARIUS	PISCES	ARIES	TAURUS	GEMINI	CANCER
20 January–18 February	19 February–20 March	21 March–20 April	21 April–20 May	21 May–20 June	21 June–21 July

Daffodils

Freesias

Tulips

Iris

Alstroemeria

Roses

Polyanthus

Cineraria

Calceolaria

Hydrangea

Pelargonium

Gloxinia

Ivy

Ferns

Monstera

Croton

Dracaena

Dieffenbachia

LEO 22 July–21 August	**VIRGO** 22 August–22 September	**LIBRA** 23 September–22 October	**SCORPIO** 23 October–21 November	**SAGITTARIUS** 22 November–20 December	**CAPRICORN** 21 December–19 January
Carnations	Gladioli	Dahlias	Gerbera	Anemones	Chrysanthemums
Begonia	Chrysanthemum	Cyclamen	African Violet	Azalea	Poinsettia
Peperomia	Philodendron	Rhoicissus	Maranta	Ficus	Mixed plants

Caring for Flowers

When buying flowers, keep their purpose in mind: those required for a dinner party are not necessarily suitable for long-term home decoration.

Look for flowers in fairly backward condition, as these will grow to their full beauty. Fully developed flowers are more suitable for use on just one occasion. With Daffodils, the neck should be turning and the buds beginning to burst. Narcissi should be firm and crisp, while Gladioli should have only two or three of their lowest flowers open. Roses should be in bud, though not tightly closed, and Tulips also should be in bud but with their natural colour well up into the petals. Carnations should be firm and crisp to the touch. With all single or daisy-shaped flowers, a centre 'eye' in green condition is a good sign.

Flowers are living things. Neglect them and they will quickly die. Different flowers have different expectations of life. Chrysanthemums, for instance, will usually last at least three weeks, while Dahlias do well if they last a week. Generally, flowers will last longer in autumn and winter, and those which are available for most of the year tend to live longer than those which are with us for only a short season.

Flowers prefer cool, airy rooms to stuffy, overheated places. Humidity is important too. The dry atmosphere of central heating bears no relation to the kindly humidity of a greenhouse. Best humidifiers for centrally-heated homes are green foliage house plants.

Carnations are highly susceptible to close, oppressive and thundery conditions. Never keep them close to fruit, as this gives off ethylene gas which is lethal to Carnations.

Water is essential for the continued life of all flowers, cool clean water which should be left to stand for an hour or so after being drawn from the tap. This allows the free oxygen to escape. The process may be speeded up by raising the temperature of the water so that it is tepid. Premature wilting of flowers may be a result of insufficient water or a build-up of bacteria within the containers and on the stems of the flowers. Cleanliness of both water and containers is very important. Equally, it is essential that flowers be able to drink, so remove the extreme ends of the stems with a slanting or oblique cut immediately before placing them in water. Any leaves that will be immersed should also be removed. Some flowers with hard, woody stems, such as Lilac, Viburnum and some garden Roses, do not take water easily. Certain of these (and do please ask your florist which ones) will benefit from being stood for two or three minutes in about 50 mm near-boiling water. (Use a metal container, as glass might crack.)

After this arrange them in cool water.

ROSES
Make sure that Roses get a good drink before arranging them. Trim the stems with a slanting cut, remove the lower leaves and use lukewarm water. If they droop overnight, dip the ends of the stems in boiling water for two minutes and then return to cool water.

CARNATIONS

Cut or break a small piece from the ends of the stems so that your Carnations can drink easily. Choose a spot between the nodes, and remove lower leaves. For longest life, keep in a cool, well ventilated room.

If it is not convenient to arrange your flowers immediately you reach home, loosen the wrapping and stand them in a bucket of water until you have time to do so.

Do not place flowers in a draught and keep them away from sources of direct heat. If you put your arrangement above a hot radiator it will not last very long. Direct sunshine will hasten the development of all flowers, thus shortening their lives. Roses and Tulips are very vulnerable and will open quickly if exposed to full sunlight.

Always seek advice before you use any proprietary brand of flower food. Do not experiment with home-made stimulants.

Many flowers are heavy drinkers. Deep water is not essential for them, but vases should be checked and topped up daily if you cannot make a complete change of water. If you are using a flower foam as a support, make sure that it is kept well soaked or has water at the base.

The golden rule with flowers is *always avoid extremes*. Remember that the world's most beautiful, longest-lasting flowers grow in the temperate zones, not in the Arctic or in the Sahara! And remember too that, like all living things, flowers must be cared for and that once they are in your possession you are the only person who can give this care.

CHRYSANTHEMUM

Break or trim off the ends of the stems with an oblique cut so that the Chrysanthemums can take water easily, and remove any leaves that will be immersed. Handle blooms with care and they will give you pleasure for at least three weeks.

GLADIOLI

Trim off the ends of the stems and remove any foliage that will be immersed in water. As the lower florets pass their prime, remove them so that the upper buds can open easily.

13

GERBERA

Give the Gerbera a long drink before making an arrangement, first removing the ends of the stems. Support the heads if the stems seem a little limp – they will soon stiffen up to their full glory.

IRIS

Trim off the ends of the stems, removing particularly the slender white extremity and any foliage which might be immersed. Often a second bud will develop if you take off the faded flower and loosen slightly the sheath which protects the buds.

ALSTROEMERIA

Remove the extreme ends of the stems with an oblique cut and also any foliage which might be immersed. These flowers have a long life, even in warm weather, but should not be exposed to direct sunshine.

FREESIA

Purchase Freesias with an open flower and several buds on each stem. Trim the ends of the stems so that they can take water easily.

NARCISSUS AND DAFFODILS

Remove the ends of the stems with an oblique cut. Stand the flowers in water for an hour or so before making an arrangement. If possible buy Daffodils with the buds just beginning to break.

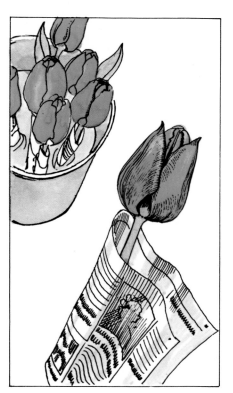

TULIPS

Trim the stems and remove leaves that may become immersed. If the stems seem limp, wrap them in newspaper and stand them in deep water for a few hours in a cool place. Purchase when the flowers are in bud, but with the colour beginning to flood up into the flower.

ANEMONES

Remove the ends of the stems so that the flowers can drink. Should they remain limp, trim them again and stand them in deep water for an hour or so. Keep as cool as possible and remove to a cool room at night.

STOCKS

Remove the whitish ends of the stems with a slanting cut. If the stems are very hard, bruise them gently by tapping them with a wooden mallet. Keep away from direct sunshine.

15

Caring for Plants

BEGONIA REX
The Begonia requires strong daylight and will enjoy diffused sunshine. Keep the soil evenly moist without over-watering. Apply diluted liquid fertilizer regularly throughout spring and summer.

Plants growing outdoors rely upon natural elements for their needs. Indoors, by contrast, they depend entirely upon you to provide them with their requirements – water, food and light.

After purchase, give your plants a quiet settling-in period. Keep them out of direct sunlight and away from draught, and be careful not to over-water them. After two weeks they can be placed in their permanent quarters and treated normally.

More plants are seriously damaged by over-watering than by any other cause. If the soil is constantly loaded with too much water, the air is driven out and the roots suffocate. So resist the temptation to give the plants a daily watering 'just to make sure'. Use the tips of your fingers as a guide – if they are moist or even damp after touching the soil the plant needs no water. Wait until the soil is beginning to feel a little dry and crumbly to the touch – being nearly dry between waterings will actually benefit most plants. If the leaves droop slightly, then the plant needs water – now. No harm will result if this happens occasionally, but do not make a habit of it.

Water your plants well, and make sure that you thoroughly saturate the root-ball. Apply water from above by gently filling the pot to the brim two or three times. Alternatively, water from below by standing the plant for a few minutes in a bowl of water; the water should not flood over the top of the soil. The holes in the bottom of the pot will ensure full saturation. Afterwards, allow all the surplus water to drain away. Never leave a plant standing in a permanent puddle of water.

Most plants require less water in winter than in the spring and summer, and of course the needs of individual plants vary. Fleshy-leaved plants need water less often since they can store it within their own tissues. Ferns must never be allowed to dry out.

Use clean rainwater whenever possible; it is a 'must' for lime-hating plants such as Azaleas. Water which has been boiled is equally suitable after it has been cooled. Otherwise, tap water is suitable for most plants, though it will tend to leave a whitish deposit on the soil surface. Always use water at room temperature.

Though most plants are grown in greater humidity than is normal in our homes, they are well able to adapt to new climatic conditions. It helps to stand their pots on a moist medium of sand, peat or pebbles, about 12.5 mm thick, at the bottom of their saucer or outer container; this gives humidity. In warm weather sponge or spray their leaves with clean water.

House plants are well suited to home temperatures. However, if your rooms are very warm, they will grow more rapidly and will need water more often. Should your house be cold for a period, the reverse is the case – less water – and, in any period of severe conditions, none at all.

Plant food should be applied regularly in spring and summer and to a plant that is in its flowering season. Liquid fertilizer is preferable as it is easier to control the dosage. Never use at a strength greater than recommended; in fact, regular applications at half strength are preferable.

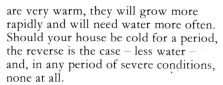

NEPHROLEPSIS FERN

As with all ferns, this should be kept moist and should never be allowed to dry out. Good light is preferable, but no sunshine. In warm weather, a gentle spray or misting with clean fresh water is very beneficial.

AECHMEA FASCIATA

This bromeliad requires steady warm conditions and should be protected from temperatures below 13°C. Large colourful blooms rise from the urn-shaped rosette of greyish downy leaves. An attractive house plant, even when not in flower, which should be watered via the leaf funnel.

17

CAMPANULA ISOPHYLLA

This attractive trailing plant is very suitable for growing in a hanging basket or on a high shelf in greenhouse or patio. It prefers coolish conditions and requires plenty of water – it should never be allowed to dry out. Flowers are blue or white. Fertilizer should be applied regularly during the flowering season.

SOLANUM (CHRISTMAS CHERRY)

These lovely orange-berried plants come to us during winter months, although they take a year to reach that condition. Keep them well watered and in as cool a room as possible. After the winter they may be planted outside, in their pots, to grow and make more berries for next autumn.

Most plants require natural daylight and will enjoy occasional exposure to diffused sunlight. Variegated foliage usually indicates a greater need for strong daylight than dark green foliage. Beware however of the damage that can be caused by direct sunshine through glass. Glass protects a plant from draughts but readily conducts heat and cold, so keep your plants away from it at seasonal extremes.

Sponge the larger-leaved plants with clean water to remove dust; this allows them to breathe and enhances their appearance.

Be alert to the effects of seasonal changes upon your plants. They will need less water in winter and little or no feeding. If re-potting is required, leave it until the spring or summer. If you take a summer holiday, stand your plants for a week or so on absorbent material in a bath or sink, with an inch of water at the bottom. The surplus water will soon trickle away, leaving the plants in confined but tolerable conditions.

Flowering plants respond very well to home conditions, and although they may flower only for a few weeks, many of them will retain gracious foliage for much of the year. Any plant in flower is at its peak and should be given every consideration in terms of water, fertilizer and servicing; remove faded blooms and foliage as they occur.

KENTIA PALM

A green plant of immense dignity, it requires good strong light but no sunshine. Water as needed; be careful not to over-water, especially in winter. Sponge the leaves regularly with clean fresh water, particularly during the summer.

CROTON

The Croton requires steady, fairly warm conditions and dislikes any kind of draught. It needs strong light but no sunshine. Its lovely colours enliven any group of house plants, and it should be kept evenly moist. Apply diluted liquid fertilizer regularly throughout the summer. Water less during winter, but never allow it to dry out.

ERICA (HEATHER)

All Ericas are thirsty and should never be allowed to become dry. They like cool conditions and are not happy in stuffy, over-heated rooms. Most are hardy and may be planted outside after flowering. Water with fresh rain water – not tap water, as these plants dislike lime.

SAINTPAULIA (AFRICAN VIOLET)

This plant requires good light, though direct sunshine should be avoided in summer. It prefers to stand on a moist medium of sand, peat or pebbles in a tray or dish. Water only when the soil seems dry, using lukewarm water for preference. Do not allow water to get on to the leaves or flowers. A humid atmosphere – over the kitchen sink or in the bathroom – is best.

POT CHRYSANTHEMUM

Apply water at room temperature as needed. The plant will enjoy a good, light position but should not be placed in direct sunshine. Remove faded flowers as they occur and plant it into the garden when it has ceased to flower. Do not buy your Chrysanthemum plant in too backward a condition, as the small green buds do not open easily indoors.

BEGONIA FIREGLOW

This plant requires strong light and will even enjoy sunshine during the winter months. Keep soil evenly moist, but avoid over-watering. While it is in flower, apply diluted fertilizer at regular intervals.

POINSETTIA

One of the loveliest and easiest plants to take home during the winter months. Keep moist but do avoid over-watering. A good light position is preferable. Apply fertilizer regularly while it is in flower.

19

Flower Arranging

The oval is made with tightly-packed flowers and is ideal for a not too spacious Victorian setting.

The formal triangle: this arrangement of massed flowers is particularly suitable on a sideboard.

The horizontal line: the accent here is on length and width, and the container should be almost hidden.

The rules are simple, but constant practice will develop your skill. If possible, always have flowers in your home; keep your eyes open to see which flowers are available and to collect ideas for home decoration.

The basic materials are wide-meshed chicken wire, a pinholder (a heavy lead base with sharp pins), a block of flower foam (a porous substance which retains water), and adhesive clay. These may be purchased at any florist's shop.

Both the wire and the foam are used to support the stems. The wire is crumpled inside the container so that it will support them at the required angles; the pin-holder should be attached to the bottom of the container with adhesive. Occasionally the two may be used together. Flower foam is a useful alternative, especially in shallow containers. It must never be crammed too tightly and should be thoroughly saturated before use. If it is to stand clear of the upper rim of the container, leave slots at the side so that water can be poured in without spillage. All fresh flowers require water which should be changed or topped up daily.

Choose a container that will not conflict with the colour scheme of your room. Build up a stock of containers, you can never have too many, and they help you to achieve variety with your arrangements.

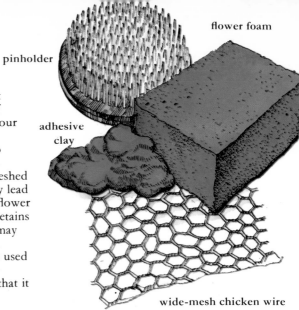

pinholder

flower foam

adhesive clay

wide-mesh chicken wire

Consider, too, the position which the arrangement will occupy. This must govern its eventual shape and size.

Flowers such as Carnations or Chrysanthemums are most suited to the more solid designs, while taller, more slender subjects such as Gladioli and Irises lend themselves to lighter, more stylized arrangements.

Colour is another important factor. A colour wheel or colour chart, obtainable from any art shop, will help tremendously in selection. Colours close in the spectrum will give gentle harmony; shades of one colour can be very restful, while drama will be achieved by the skilful balance of contrasting colours.

HOGARTH CURVE

1

2

3

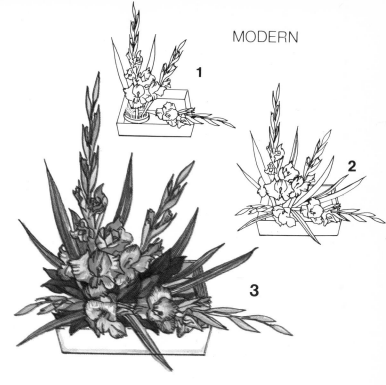

MODERN

1

2

3

Start by selecting the flower that is to indicate the dominant line and height. This is often called the 'vertical'. Place this where you want it, keeping in mind that, for correct proportion, the stem length visible should be about one and a half times the container's greatest measurement – that is its height if you are using a vase, its breadth for a bowl.

The remainder of the flowers should be so placed in the design that they seem to radiate from one central point. Stems should not cross visibly; their lengths may vary, though all should be shorter than the 'vertical'. Use suitable foliages to emphasize the shape of the design and complement the flowers.

Your arrangement should balance, visually and actually. Heavy blooms and flowers with rich bold colours are better placed towards the base of the design, often creating its focal point. Lighter blossoms and flowers of softer shades are generally more effective towards the perimeter.

Always use a container with a good stable base; choose the one most suited to your purpose, remembering that it must not in any way dominate the flowers.

Your design need not be symmetrical. A freer style with gracious curves can be just as effective.

Remember that the key is enjoyment – there is great happiness to be found in working with flowers.

21

Growing Indoor Bulbs

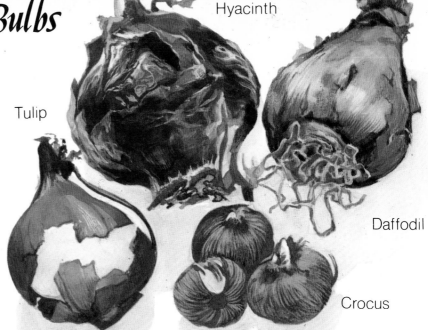

Hyacinth

Tulip

Daffodil

Crocus

It is always extremely difficult to think about the dark days of winter if you have just returned home from a summer holiday. But if you want your bulbs to flower for Christmas you should certainly buy them before the end of September. Look for those marked 'pre-cooled' or 'prepared' and plant immediately after buying them. Timing is very important for the best results – it is no use buying bulbs late and then putting them in a warm room. Bulbs which are being forced have to make a good root system before the leaves and flower stems start to grow, and this takes two or three months. For the best results, the bowls should be kept in cool, dark conditions, preferably with some ventilation – definitely not the airing cupboard!

The general rule when buying bulbs is the larger the better; they should also feel firm. Daffodil bulbs should be egg-sized (about 13 cm); they can be single-nosed (rounds) or double-nosed. Tulips should have a circumference of at least 11 cm and a diameter of 5 cm. Crocus should be not be less than 8 cm in circumference, about the size of a 2 pence coin.

If you use containers without drainage holes, you will have to grow your bulbs in one of the special bulb fibres now available; this will remain fresh throughout the growing season. Place a layer of moist fibre at the bottom of your bowl; don't press it down too hard or the new roots will not be able to penetrate. Then press the bulbs into the fibre and fill the bowl with more moist fibre so that the bulb tips are just showing; remember to leave at least 12.5 mm space for watering.

While you are storing your bulbs, do not forget to examine them regularly and to make sure that the bulb fibre is moist. If, however, it becomes too wet the bulbs will rot.

You must not be tempted to bring your bowls out into the light too soon. Wait until the buds are well out of the neck of the bulbs and at least 5 cm growth is showing. This is absolutely vital: four out of every five bulbs grown indoors die because they are brought into warmth and light too soon.

To grow Hyacinths in glasses, buy the largest bulbs, then fill the glass with water (preferably rainwater) so that it almost touches the base of the bulb and add a few pieces of charcoal to keep the water clean. Then place the glass in a cool, dark room until the sprouts are about 7.5 cm high and gradually bring it to the full light, adding water when necessary.

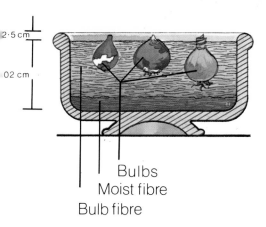

2·5 cm

·02 cm

Bulbs
Moist fibre
Bulb fibre

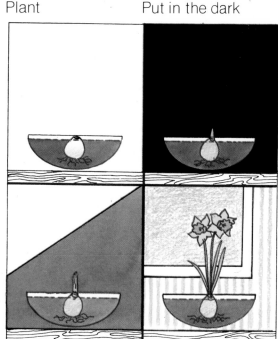

Plant   Put in the dark

Put in the shade   Put in the light

Once you have brought your bulbs out into the light, keep them in a cool, shady position; never put them in a warm, light place until their flowers are visible. If after two or three days the shoots do not appear to be growing, return the bulbs to their previous cool dark conditions; then, a week or ten days later, test them once again.

When you are sure they are thriving, the bulbs can be moved to wherever you wish them to flower, but keep them away from direct heat and draughts and remember to turn the bowls occasionally to prevent uneven growth.

To keep foliage dwarf and to assist good colouring of the flowers, give the bulbs an occasional supply of liquid fertilizer during the growth period.

When your bulbs have finished flowering, first cut off the old flower heads and then plant them in the garden for a display the following year. Forced bulbs cannot be grown in bowls for more than one season.

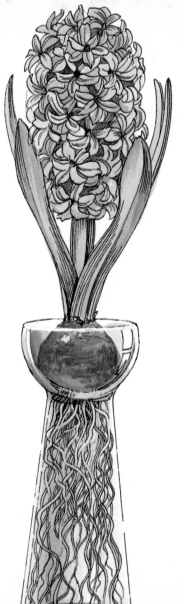

23

Bedding Plants

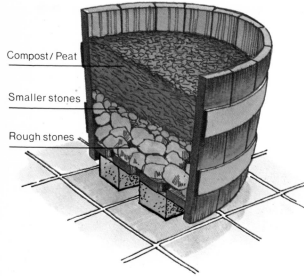

Compost/Peat

Smaller stones

Rough stones

Window boxes, tubs and hanging baskets mean that today everyone can be a gardener.

Choosing suitable containers must be the first step – and that really depends on your own preference. Once you have fixed on something, your choice of plant will be determined by the amount of light which the container receives.

Fill the container with a growing material: peat- and sand-based materials are entirely suitable, and the well-tried John Innes compost can also be used if a reliable source can be found (John Innes No. 2 or its equivalent includes the appropriate amount of fertilizer). Remember to

avoid materials with lime if you have chosen plants such as heathers or azaleas.

Good drainage is a first consideration whatever the growing medium. Fill the bottom half of large containers with rough stones. A layer of smaller stones placed on top will prevent the compost sifting down. Do not fill right to the rim and leave room for watering.

Baskets never seem to have enough compost to sustain their plants. Old-style wire baskets lined with moss dry out very quickly if left hanging in sun and wind, and although the moss is pleasing in appearance it acts as a wick and accelerates drying, so only use it if

you are prepared for constant attention. A plastic lining overcomes the problem – but in that case you might as well settle for plastic hanging baskets, which are cheaper. Some manufacturers add a saucer underneath the basket which acts as a reservoir. It also prevents the basket dripping, so long as you do not overfill it.

Practically anything can be grown in a container if it is large – and you are determined – enough, but the most satisfactory subjects for your summer display are bound to include many old favourites. These have been immensely improved by the introduction of new strains of seed in the past few years. Look out for the new seedling Geraniums. These are very free flowering singles and are obtainable in all colours. There is also a wide range of the improved, but slightly more expensive, double Geraniums. The Ivy Geranium is indispensable around the edges of containers, as is the Trailing Fuchsia.

Petunias can blow their own trumpets. The largest ones need some protection from wind and rain and require all the sun that they can find; the smaller ones will tolerate rather less shelter. The F1 hybrid strains will repay the extra cost and can be purchased in flower in individual containers and transferred straightaway to their new situation. This also applies

to French Marigolds which increase in variety every year. The larger crested ones are strongly recommended and flower freely well into the autumn.

If a riot of colour is not to your taste, add foliage plants – the grey Cineraria Maritima or the darker variegated leaves of Coleus – to produce subtle effects.

These plants will do well in sunny situations. In less sunny but protected places Impatiens (which you may know as Busy Lizzie) will thrive. It can be obtained in many colours and on its own, either mixed or in just one colour, it will fill an eye-catching tub or basket.

You can also grow Impatiens in a pillar. Line a cylinder of strong wire netting with polythene and fill it with compost. Then make holes in the polythene and insert the plants both round the circumference and up and down the lengths. Once it starts growing you will see nothing but flowers.

Begonias also prefer some shade but cannot stand cold rain or wind. The small flowering plants are tougher than the double flower tuberous varieties.

Trailing Lobelia can be obtained in a number of colours for edging. Alyssum can also be used, but it cannot be seen in a hanging basket above head height. The new strains of Ageratum and the Calceolaria 'Summer Sunshine' are interestingly different in colour and form.

Unless your container is large, avoid tall subjects, but you might find it worth trying Zinnia or African Marigold to increase the height in the centre of a large tub.

Remember that when you grow plants in containers you usually end up with a high density of root, foliage and flower. Feed a general liquid fertilizer in small quantities, and if you remove the seed heads the flowering period will be prolonged until the first frosts.

Cacti and Succulents

Cacti and Succulents have a unique fascination. Their forms are invariably interesting; some are beautiful, many strange, yet others grotesque – and all tell of the amazing adaptability of plant life.

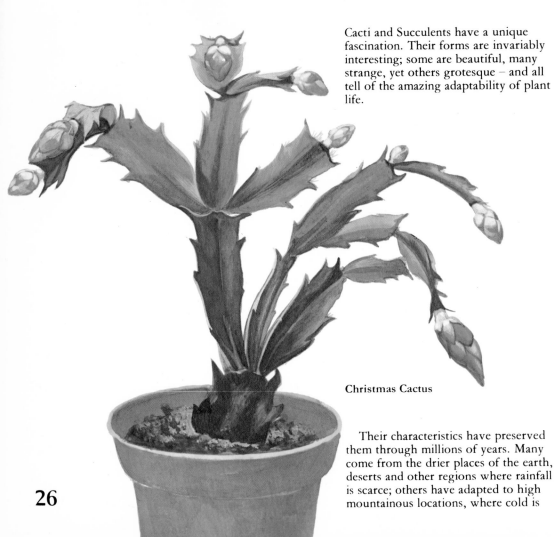

Christmas Cactus

Their characteristics have preserved them through millions of years. Many come from the drier places of the earth, deserts and other regions where rainfall is scarce; others have adapted to high mountainous locations, where cold is their chief enemy, and a third group have their home in tropical forests, where they may be found high up in trees, rooted to the bark.

All this means that these plants are very tolerant of house conditions, especially where a dry atmosphere prevails. They can take a degree of neglect that would kill many house plants and will even thrive on it.

True Cacti are but one form of Succulent. Many bear spines; their form can vary from the elongated and rope-like Hylocereanae (or Forest Cereus) to the strange, urn-like shapes of the Mammillarias. Stems sometimes look more like leaves, but the leaved Cactus is rare. Other varieties bear no thorns at all. Many varieties will flower, given the right conditions.

All Cacti and Succulents have one characteristic in common – their unique ability to conserve moisture within their own structure, so that they can exist without rain or watering for long periods.

Most Cacti and Succulents have an annual growing and resting cycle. They respond to light, temperature and water in varying ways. Generally their most active period is in the spring and summer, and they slow down in the autumn to relative dormancy in winter. They should be given plenty of water in their growing season and dry, cool conditions in winter.

Partridge Breast Aloe

Black-spice Prickly Pear

Variegated Caribbean Agave

Mammillaria

When applying water, be sure to saturate the root-ball thoroughly; then wait until the soil begins to feel dry before watering again. Never over-water the plant, as its roots must breathe between waterings, and never stand it in a puddle of water. In winter many varieties can be left quite dry.

Allow varieties which flower in the winter to grow freely in spring and early summer, and then give them a dry period until about two months before they are expected to flower. Normal watering can then be resumed; once the buds have formed, however, move the plant as little as possible as variations of light can cause bud-drop.

Most plants require strong daylight and will flourish best in windows which face south. Exceptions are the winter-flowering varieties which require only moderate light and are better without direct sunlight.

You do not need hot rooms in order to keep Cacti and Succulents. Most will require moderate temperatures at the most (about 15 to 18°C); a cool greenhouse or veranda is often ideal during the summer months. Some plants will enjoy a summer with their pots bedded into the ground in some sheltered spot in the garden. Fertilizer should be applied during the growing season, but never during the dry periods. Apply a liquid or water-soluble fertilizer with strong phsophoric content regularly and in well diluted doses.

27

Flowers in the Home

There is one place in our lives where flowers can really be enjoyed – at home, where we have time to enjoy their fragrance and beauty.

These few suggestions will help to enhance your home.

Table arrangements should complement, not dominate, a table. The flowers should not impede your view of the person sitting opposite, nor should the foliage entangle itself with the food. Smaller flowers and those of firm, erect habit are often most suitable, though spring flowers in a mixed arrangement can be particularly charming. Make your arrangement in a foam base and put it on a small plate or a piece of foil just in case it stains the cloth or a polished table.

Gift arrangements are very often 'faced' or sideboard arrangements. Put them away from draughts in reasonable light. Top up the container with water, and check daily that they have not dried out. When some of the flowers fade, replace them with others or perhaps with foliage from the garden. When the whole arrangement is finished, clean out the container and keep it for future use.

Flowers can often be 'lost' if placed against bold, multi-coloured wall coverings. By contrast, they will enhance a plain wall or a corner without other features. They do not need to be placed close to a window; in fact it is better to put them on the further side of the room, but facing the light. Do not place them over a radiator or on a mantelpiece over a fire, as the warm air will make them deteriorate quickly.

If you use one room at home as an office, green plants can do much to relieve its austerity. Two or three are usually sufficient, including one miniature plant or a small bowl of flowers on the main table. Flowers can break tension and provide a talking point, even with the most nervous client.

Flowers in the hall say welcome very clearly, provided they are cared for and are not allowed to wilt in a draught. Frankly, entrance halls are difficult places for flowers, and a fairly hardy plant such as a Fatsia or a Shefflera may be the best answer. Small plants give a great deal of pleasure to their owners and to visitors: the tray of African Violets on a window-sill over the kitchen sink, the pots of Begonias blazing with colour on a cottage window ledge, a collection of Impatiens (Busy Lizzie) plants in a tiny lean-to greenhouse – all of these are the little delights of having flowers about the house.

If you have a guest coming for the weekend a small choice arrangement of flowers on the dressing-table or beside the bed will say welcome in the nicest way.

House plants can be displayed with grand effect in hanging containers, often made of plastic fibres or string. These can be used in almost any part of the house and are particularly attractive in open-plan apartments. Make sure that the plants receive sufficient light. For the best results choose plants which prefer to hang or trail, such as the Grape Ivy, various kinds of Hedera and the Chlorophytum (Spider Plant).

Even the relatively austere decor of many bathrooms can be relieved by a few moisture-loving plants, such as African Violets, Ficus Pumila and various dainty ferns.

29

This chart shows when selected flowers are most plentiful ★ when there is general availability ☆ and when they are least available ○ in the United States.

NOTE: This chart was prepared for Florists' Transworld Delivery and is based on an analysis of market reporting information published by the United States Department of Agriculture. The information is intended as a guideline only.

	JAN	FEB	MAR
Long-Stemmed Roses	☆	○	☆
Sweetheart Roses	☆	○	☆
Standard Size Carnations	☆	○	☆
Miniature Carnations	☆	☆	★
Large Chrysanthemums	○	☆	☆
Pompons	☆	○	☆
Gladioli	☆	☆	☆
Iris	○	☆	★
Snapdragons	☆	☆	☆
Marguerite Daisies	★	☆	☆
Majestic Daisies	☆	★	☆
Anemones	○	○	☆
Bulb Flowers (some varieties)	★	★	★
Bird of Paradise (imported)	★	★	★

APRIL	MAY	JUNE	JULY	AUG	SEPT	OCT	NOV	DEC
☆	☆	★	★	★	☆	☆	☆	☆
☆	☆	☆	★	★	☆	★	☆	☆
☆	☆	☆	★	★	★	★	★	☆
○	☆	☆	★	★	★	☆	☆	○
☆	☆	★	★	★	★	☆	☆	☆
☆	☆	☆	★	★	★	★	☆	☆
☆	☆	★	★	★	★	☆	☆	☆
☆	★	★	☆	★	☆	☆	☆	○
○	☆	☆	★	★	☆	☆	★	☆
☆	☆	☆	★	★	★	★	☆	☆
☆	☆	☆	★	★	☆	○	○	☆
☆	☆	★	☆	☆	★	★	☆	★
☆	☆	☆	☆	☆	☆	☆	☆	☆
★	★	☆	☆	○	○	☆	☆	☆

31

Remembrance

REMEMBRANCE

Flowers are a traditional way of demonstrating respect for the dead and sympathy for the bereaved. Whether a funeral tribute or a gift of flowers to the bereaved family, flowers will convey your message of love and understanding and will help to express your innermost feelings.

When words fail, flowers are the visual expression of what we wish to say.

A basket of Roses, Gladioli and Freesias, equally suitable for a funeral or as a gift to the family of the deceased.

A wreath of lovely seasonal flowers, the traditional symbol of eternity.

A formal cross of white Chrysanthemums, with spray of Roses and Lilies: the emblem of Christianity.

32

Acknowledgments

The authors would like to thank the following people who advised and assisted in the preparation of this book: Rona Coleman, S.F. (Dip.), A.I.F.D.; Lydia Grogan; A.M. Jansen, senior; Eric Roberts, M.S.A. (Dip.); Angus Valentine; and Alan A. Wood.

Created, designed and produced by Ventura Publishing Limited, 44 Uxbridge Street London W8 7TG

Copyright © Ventura Publishing Ltd, London, 1979

First English edition published by Arthur Barker Limited, London, in 1979.

This edition is published by Avenel Books, a division of Crown Publishers, Inc.

Library of Congress Catalog Card Number: 79-3956

Filmsetting by Filmtype Services Ltd, Scarborough, Yorks.
Colour Separations by Colour Workshop Ltd, Hertford, Herts.

Printed in England by Penshurst Press Ltd, Tunbridge Wells, Kent